First Grade Homework

Real-Life Activities that Turn Homework into Family Fun

Written by Karen Bauer and Rosa Drew

Illustrated by Ann Iosa

Edited by Vicky Shiotsu

Project Managed by Sue Lewis

Project Directed by Carolea Williams

Table of Contents

Introduction

First-grade children are eager and ready to learn. These enthusiastic young students enjoy age-appropriate homework assignments that provide successful learning experiences. The home offers many opportunities to make learning come alive. For example, when a family prepares meals together, holds discussions during dinner, or plans outings, children interact in real-life situations that make learning meaningful. Positive homework or "homeplay" lays the foundation for good work habits in later years and involves parents as partners in their children's daily learning experiences.

First Grade Homework

- includes creative activities that transform homework into "homeplay"—a positive, exciting, and creative experience for first-grade students.

- provides ready-to-use reproducibles requiring almost no teacher-preparation time.

- empowers parents with information and practical ideas they can implement easily as they become partners in their child's education.

- gives the whole family the opportunity to be part of the homework process.

- describes techniques that parents can use to help their children establish the good work habits essential for successful learning.

- offers teachers a choice of how to present homework to students, giving them the flexibility to tailor the methods to meet students' needs.

Types of Homework Activities

Design your own homework program by choosing from the following types of activities included in *First Grade Homework*.

Monthly Calendars

Twelve monthly calendars with five learning activities per week are provided. Parents and children can complete a specific number of activities each week and then complete a response journal designed for the month. A blank calendar is also provided so you can design your own activities.

Monthly Celebrations

An activity following a seasonal theme is provided for each month of the year. Invite parents and students to complete the monthly celebrations and then return a record of the celebration to school.

Fun With Short Vowels

Two pages for each short vowel are provided. The first page presents activities that reinforce auditory discrimination; the second page presents activities that give practice in reading and writing. A review page of the five short vowels is provided at the back of this section. A variety of activities are listed on each page so that children and parents can choose which ones they want to complete.

Across the Curriculum

Engaging homework activities are presented for language arts, math, science, social studies, music, art, drama, and physical education. Easy-to-follow directions lead children and parents through each step in the activity. Send these activities home to correlate with a current topic of study or a thematic unit.

Family Adventures

Family adventures are designed for students and their entire families to enjoy. Families are invited to experience both real and imaginary adventures. Several suggestions are offered for each adventure so children and parents can choose how they will complete the homework.

Timely Tips Newsletters

The reproducible newsletters provide parents with information to help make their child's learning experience at home even more productive. Topics include homework tips, reading, television-viewing, learning on the go, and building a child's self-confidence. Send the newsletters home throughout the year with your regular classroom newsletter to keep parents informed.

October Response Journal

Help your child complete this page. Turn in this journal along with the calendar on the last school day of October.

Student

1. My favorite activity was _____ .

   I liked it because _____

   _____ .

2. One activity I needed help with was _____

   _____ .

3. I learned _____

   _____ .

Parent

1. I learned _____ .

2. The activity I most enjoyed doing with my child was _____

   _____ .

3. The activity I helped my child with most was _____

   _____ .

Parent's Signature _____

Name _____

Choose at least _____ activities to complete each week. Check the box in the lower right corner of each calendar square as your child completes the activity. Turn in the calendar and the response journal on the last school day of November.

November

Monday	Tuesday	Wednesday	Thursday	Friday
Count the seeds in a pumpkin.	Americans vote for a president every four years. Who is the president right now?	Go to the polls with your parents on Election Day.	Find a store ad in the news-paper. Does the ad make you want to visit the store? Explain.	Tell what you know about the first Thanksgiving.
Have an adult help you roast pumpkin seeds using margarine and seasoned salt.	Read a story. Name the main characters and describe them.	Write to your favorite author. Tell why you like his or her book.	Write your first and last name. Count the letters. Which name has more letters?	Count to 100 by fives.
Get five pumpkin seeds. Use them to help you write addition facts for 5.	How many letters are in *November*? How many are in *October*? What is the difference?	Count backwards from 20 to 1. 20,19,18,	Write the alpha-bet in lowercase letters. Circle the vowels.	Read a poetry book. Memorize a poem.
Name the months that have 30 days.	What is a vet-eran? Do you know anyone who served in the Armed Forces?	Get 10 dimes. Show 20¢. Show 50¢. Show 90¢.	Take a walk. Look for seeds or seed pods. Glue or tape them to a piece of card-board.	Write what you would do on Thanksgiving if you were a turkey.
Draw a turkey using circles, ovals, rectangles, and triangles.	As a family, talk about the things for which you are thankful.	Help with Thanksgiving preparations.	Describe how you and your family celebrate Thanksgiving.	Make a calendar for December. Write in the special days.

March Response Journal

Help your child complete this page. Turn in this journal along with the calendar on the last school day of March.

Student

1. My favorite activity was _____ .

   I liked it because _____

   _____ .

2. One activity I needed help with was _____

   _____ .

3. I learned _____

   _____ .

Parent

1. I learned _____ .

2. The activity I most enjoyed doing with my child was _____

   _____ .

3. The activity I helped my child with most was _____

   _____ .

Parent's Signature _____

Name _____

Choose at least _____ activities to complete each week. Check the box in the lower right corner of each calendar square as your child completes the activity. Turn in the calendar and the response journal on the last school day of April.

 # April

Monday	Tuesday	Wednesday	Thursday	Friday
Try to trick a friend with a riddle.	Visit your library. Find three different things you can borrow.	Count 30 pieces of macaroni by ones. Then count them by twos, threes, fives, and tens.	Take a walk with your family. Take a bag and collect three nonliving things.	Bounce a ball with your right hand and then with your left. Which is easier?
Discuss the saying *April showers bring May flowers.*	Name five animals and their babies. (dog, puppy) Which baby is your favorite?	Name five words that have a short e sound (as in *hen*).	Talk with your family about ways you can save energy and recycle.	Find things in your home that begin with *ch*, *th*, and *sh*.
Using 5, 3, and 8, write two addition facts and two subtraction facts.	If each vowel in your name is worth five cents, how much money is your name worth?	Use dimes, nickels, and pennies to show 19¢, 34¢, 46¢, and 82¢.	Use a ruler to measure four objects. Draw a picture of each object and write its length.	Tell about something kind you did for someone. How did the two of you feel?
Write the names of the oldest and youngest members of your family.	Line up your shoes. Count them by twos.	Count by fives to 100. Write the numbers.	Tell how spring is different from winter.	Name four ways animals move.
Read a story. Who was your favorite character? Tell someone why.	Write five words that rhyme with *spring*.	Discuss with your family the things you find funny.	Make a list of six products that are made from wood.	Write the two words that make up each of these contractions: *didn't, isn't, can't.*

April Response Journal

Help your child complete this page. Turn in this journal along with the calendar on the last school day of April.

Student

1. My favorite activity was _____ .

   I liked it because _____

   _____ .

2. One activity I needed help with was _____

   _____ .

3. I learned _____

   _____ .

Parent

1. I learned _____ .

2. The activity I most enjoyed doing with my child was _____

   _____ .

3. The activity I helped my child with most was _____

   _____ .

Parent's Signature _____

Name _____

Choose at least _____ activities to complete each week. Check the box in the lower right corner of each calendar square as your child completes the activity. Turn in the calendar and the response journal on the last school day of May.

May

Monday	Tuesday	Wednesday	Thursday	Friday
Visit a pet store. How many dogs and cats are there? Write a math fact to show the total.	Say the name of your street, city, state, and country.	Look at a May calendar. How many dates have a 7 in the ones place? (Example: May 27)	Look at some family photos. Have each family member share his or her favorite photo.	Design a bookmark for May.
Talk about pet care. Write two things that every pet needs.	Go on a family bike ride. Practice safety rules.	Use a ball to play catch with a partner.	Make a list of words that rhyme with *May*.	Estimate how far you can run in one minute. Then try it.
Choose a flower. See if you can find these parts: stem, leaf, petals, stamen, pistil.	Using 5, 4, and 9, write two addition facts and two subtraction facts.	Draw a row of flowers showing a pattern.	Find out your height and your weight.	Figure out in what year you will turn ten years old.
Plant flower seeds in a pot or a garden.	Estimate how many circles you can draw in one minute? Now try it.	Play outdoors with a family member or friend.	Play some music. Make up a dance for it.	Discuss the meaning of Memorial Day with your family.
Name five animals that have scales.	Make a special card for Mom for Mother's Day.	Name as many flowers as you can.	Read a story to someone.	Visit a local nursery. Look at the flowers. Later, draw a picture of a flower you saw.

May Response Journal

Help your child complete this page. Turn in this journal along with the calendar on the last school day of May.

Student

1. My favorite activity was _____.

   I liked it because _____

   _____.

2. One activity I needed help with was _____

   _____.

3. I learned _____

   _____.

Parent

1. I learned _____.

2. The activity I most enjoyed doing with my child was _____

   _____.

3. The activity I helped my child with most was _____

   _____.

Parent's Signature _____

Name _____

Choose at least _____ activities to complete each week. Check the box in the lower right corner of each calendar square as your child completes the activity. Turn in the calendar and the response journal on the last school day of June.

 # June

Monday	Tuesday	Wednesday	Thursday	Friday
Look at a June calendar. How many dates have a 2 in the tens place? (Example: June 26)	Use *left* and *right* as you direct someone from a bedroom to the kitchen.	Draw pictures of four things that begin with *ch*.	Teach a song to a family member or friend.	Estimate how many windows are in your home. Then count them.
Write what time your school begins and ends. How long are you in school?	Count by ones from 50 to 100.	Each star on the U.S. flag stands for a state. Name as many states as you can.	Write a thank-you note to your teacher for helping you this year.	Make a card for your dad or grandfather for Father's Day. Tell why he is special to you.
Make your own phone book. Have friends add their phone numbers.	Look at a road map. Find roads, freeways, cities, and water.	Count the U.S. flag's red and white stripes. Write how many stripes there are of each color.	Look up your school in a phone book.	Glue ten toothpicks onto paper to make an interesting design.
Using 6, 4, and 10, write two addition facts and two subtraction facts.	Discuss things you can do now that you couldn't do earlier in the school year.	Write three things you want to do this summer.	Look in the newspaper to find the times for sunrise and sunset today.	Name three animals that sleep in the daytime and are active at night.
Read or tell a story to someone younger than you.	Write all the math facts you can think of that have 10 as the answer.	Draw a map of your bedroom showing a bird's-eye view.	Draw a picture of yourself having fun in the summer.	How many compound words can you make with *sun*?

June Response Journal

Help your child complete this page. Turn in this journal along with the calendar on the last school day of June.

Student

1. My favorite activity was _____.

   I liked it because _____

   _____.

2. One activity I needed help with was _____

   _____.

3. I learned _____

   _____.

Parent

1. I learned _____.

2. The activity I most enjoyed doing with my child was _____

   _____.

3. The activity I helped my child with most was _____

   _____.

Parent's Signature _____

Name _____

Choose at least _____ activities to complete each week. Check the box in the lower right corner of each calendar square as your child completes the activity. Turn in the calendar and the response journal on the last school day of July.

July

Monday	Tuesday	Wednesday	Thursday	Friday
Make a banner for July the Fourth. Display the banner in your room.	Play shadow tag with a friend.	Suppose you could create a new flavor of ice cream. What would it be?	Get a refrigerator magnet. Find five objects it will pick up and five objects it won't.	Act out a nursery rhyme without speaking. See if your family can guess the rhyme.
Choose a book. How many words in the title can you spell by yourself?	List the months that have 31 days.	How many ways can you make 78¢ with dimes, nickels, and pennies?	What time does your favorite TV program begin and end? Draw two clocks to show your answer.	Compare the seeds of three fruits or vegetables. Draw pictures of the seeds and label them.
Call a friend and compare what you have been doing.	Arrange shells or buttons to make a pattern.	Name five things that can melt.	Put a puzzle together with your family.	Draw a picture of your family. Show the members from the tallest to the shortest.
How many patriotic songs does your family know?	Do you have more doors or windows in your home? Count to find out.	Draw an ocean scene. Include at least four different animals.	Plan a family picnic. List the items you'll need.	Make something using empty boxes and containers.
Read *Peter Rabbit*. Make a picture of Mr. McGregor's garden.	Experiment with objects to see if they sink or float.	Write the even numbers from 2 to 20 on the sidewalk with chalk.	Go on a picnic or eat a meal outside.	Go outside and close your eyes for two minutes. What sounds do you hear?

July Response Journal

Help your child complete this page. Turn in this journal along with the calendar on the last school day of July.

Student

1. My favorite activity was _____ .

   I liked it because _____

   _____ .

2. One activity I needed help with was _____

   _____ .

3. I learned _____

   _____ .

Parent

1. I learned _____ .

2. The activity I most enjoyed doing with my child was _____

   _____ .

3. The activity I helped my child with most was _____

   _____ .

Parent's Signature _____

Choose at least _____ activities to complete each week. Check the box in the lower right corner of each calendar square as your child completes the activity. Turn in the calendar and the response journal on the last school day of August.

August

Monday	Tuesday	Wednesday	Thursday	Friday
Look in the weather section of the newspaper. Circle today's high and low temperatures.	Begin with 22 and count to 50.	Write with water on the sidewalk using a paint-brush.	Read a book. Who is the author? Who is the illustrator?	Make up a game and teach it to your family.
Drape a blanket or an old sheet over a table to make a tent. Crawl inside and read a book.	Read a fairy tale. Make a map showing where the main events take place.	List ten liquids that are found in your home.	Talk about ways people keep cool in hot weather. Try one or more of these ideas.	Look at the stars tonight. Can you find the Big Dipper?
Balance on one foot and then on the other foot. Is one foot easier to balance on than the other?	Go outside and look at the clouds. Draw two shapes you see.	Write a postcard and send it to a relative or friend.	Name five things that make you think of school.	Play in a sprinkler. Look for rainbows in the water.
Make juice cubes by filling an ice cube tray with juice. Freeze.	Draw clocks to show the times you eat breakfast, lunch, and dinner.	Trace around three small objects on paper. Ask someone to identify the shapes.	Play tic-tac-toe with someone.	List different ways you could travel to school.
Make a "cool" picture using cool colors (blue, green, purple).	Show three ways you can make one dollar using coins.	Make a list of words that rhyme with *hot*.	Write your first and last name. Trace over the letters with different colors to make a design.	Make a musical instrument using things found in your home.

August Response Journal

Help your child complete this page. Turn in this journal along with the calendar on the last school day of August.

Student

1. My favorite activity was _____.

    I liked it because _____

    _____.

2. One activity I needed help with was _____

    _____.

3. I learned _____

    _____.

Parent

1. I learned _____.

2. The activity I most enjoyed doing with my child was _____

    _____.

3. The activity I helped my child with most was _____

    _____.

Parent's Signature _____

Monday	Tuesday	Wednesday	Thursday	Friday

To the teacher: Use this calendar for any month. Write your own activities.

Monthly Celebrations

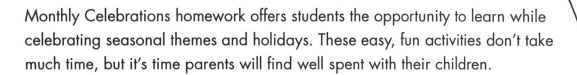

Monthly Celebrations homework offers students the opportunity to learn while celebrating seasonal themes and holidays. These easy, fun activities don't take much time, but it's time parents will find well spent with their children.

Send home the Monthly Celebrations homework at the beginning of the month. The homework includes two simple activity choices for children to complete alone or with family members. Children and parents can choose just one activity—the one they feel is most appropriate. Ask children to complete the activity anytime during the month. Encourage parents to help as needed.

The directions on the page ask parents to record their child's responses to the activity at the bottom of the page. Children should return the homework page on the last school day of the month.

You can use the July and August Homework Celebrations for summer homework or in year-round schools. Page 44 can be used at any time during the year.

Choose one activity. When it is completed, help your child dictate responses as you write them down at the bottom of the page. Return this page on the last school day of September.

1. A Leaf Hunt

Discuss the changes that occur in fall. Take a walk around your neighborhood and collect a variety of leaves. Sort the leaves by shape, size, or color. Then look at the edges of each leaf. Are the edges smooth, toothed, or lobed? Sort the leaves by their edges.

Next, arrange some leaves between two sheets of wax paper. Cover with newspaper. Ask an adult to press a warm iron over the paper to make a leaf collage. Tape the collage to a window.

2. Family Time Capsule

Have each family member fill out a paper listing his or her name, age, height, and weight. Each person should also include a goal for the year and information about favorite foods, books, music, and TV programs. Place the papers in a box or a bag along with recent family photos. Add a newspaper showing the current date. Label the container with your family name. Put the Time Capsule away for a year. Mark on a calendar when your family will open the capsule and compare the growth and changes that have taken place.

Tell about the activity. What did you like about it?

_____   _____

_____

_____

Parent's Signature _____

Choose one activity. When it is completed, help your child dictate responses as you write them down at the bottom of the page. Return this page on the last school day of October.

1. Skeleton Poster

Look in a library book or an encyclopedia to find out about the human skeleton. Study an X-ray picture if you have one. Talk about the different bones in the body. Then lie on a long sheet of brown wrapping paper (the kind used for mailing packages). Ask an adult to trace around your body. Afterwards, work together to draw in the skeleton. Label these parts: skull, collarbone, ribs, hand, hip, femur, knee, foot.

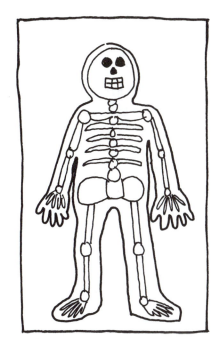

2. Fire-Safety Check

Take a tour of your home and check for the following:

- ☐ smoke detectors that work
- ☐ furnace and water heater areas that are clear
- ☐ fire extinguishers
- ☐ two escape routes for every room
- ☐ every family member's ability to call for help
- ☐ every family member's ability to state address and phone number
- ☐ evacuation plan in case of fire

Tell about the activity you chose. What did you like about it?

_____

_____

_____

Parent's Signature _____

Choose one activity. When it is completed, help your child dictate responses as you write them down at the bottom of the page. Return this page on the last school day of November.

1. Sharing With Others

Discuss the meaning of Thanksgiving with your family and have each person name one thing for which he or she is thankful. Talk about the first Thanksgiving feast and the foods that the Pilgrims and Native Americans shared with each other; such as turkeys, ducks, deer, fish, and corn. Then prepare a food basket to share with people who have less than you. Deliver the basket to a local food pantry.

2. Apple Turkey

Make a turkey you can eat! You will need an apple, 9 or 10 toothpicks, 5 gumdrops (one should be red), raisins, and 16 miniature marshmallows.

1. Insert four toothpicks into the apple to support the fruit.

2. Make four tail feathers. For each feather, poke a toothpick through four marshmallows and one gumdrop. Insert the toothpicks into one end of the apple.

3. For the neck, poke one toothpick through several raisins. Add a red gumdrop for the head. Insert the toothpick into the apple.

4. Break a small piece off a toothpick. Use it to attach a raisin onto the gumdrop for the wattle. Break off two more toothpick pieces and use them to attach a raisin on each side of the head for eyes.

Tell about the activity. What did you like about it?

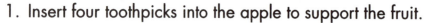

_____

_____

_____

Parent's Signature _____

Choose one activity. When it is completed, help your child dictate responses as you write them down at the bottom of the page. Return this page on the last school day of December.

1. Memory Wreath

Cut out a large paper circle. Cut out the middle of the circle to form a wreath. Draw a bow at the top of the wreath and write the year underneath it. Then share special memories of the past year. Include events such as birthday celebrations, vacations, and weekend outings. List the memories around the wreath. Display your wreath for all to enjoy.

2. New Year's Eve Cake

Make a clock cake to ring in the new year. Get a cake mix and bake it in a round pan. When cool, cover the cake with white frosting. Then place 12 round chocolate wafers around the top of the cake for the clock's numbers. Use a tube of colored frosting to write the numbers on the wafers. Use the tube to draw the hands to show midnight. Eat the cake on New Year's Eve or New Year's Day.

Tell about the activity you chose. What did you like about it?

_____

_____

_____

Parent's Signature _____

Choose one activity. When it is completed, help your child dictate responses as you write them down at the bottom of the page. Return this page on the last school day of January.

1. Homemade Frost

Frost is made up of ice crystals and forms on very cold surfaces. Make some frost at home! You will need an empty coffee can, some ice cubes, rock salt, and a magnifying glass. First, fill the coffee can with a layer of ice cubes. Then add a thick layer of rock salt. Alternate layers of ice cubes and rock salt until the can is full. Use twice as much ice as salt. Check the can in 30 minutes. With your finger, scrape some crystals off the side of the can and place them on a dark surface. Examine the crystals with a magnifying glass.

2. Bird Feeder

Make a bird feeder to help your feathered friends during the winter months. Cut two rectangular openings about two inches from the bottom of a capped two-liter plastic bottle. One opening should be at the front of the bottle and the other at the back. Then ask an adult to poke a wire through the neck of the bottle, just under the cap. Fill the bottom of the bottle with birdseed. Hang the feeder on a tree branch. Twist the ends of the wire together to secure.

Tell about the activity. What did you like about it?

_____

_____

_____

Parent's Signature _____

Choose one activity. When it is completed, help your child dictate responses as you write them down at the bottom of the page. Return this page on the last school day of February.

1. Valentine Greetings

Cut out different sizes and colors of paper hearts. Then create designs, animals, and flowers with your hearts. Glue them onto folded paper to make colorful greeting cards. Write a message inside each card and deliver your valentine greetings to a nursing home, a hospital, or a senior citizens' center.

2. Lincoln and Washington Booklets

Americans celebrate the birthdays of presidents George Washington and Abraham Lincoln in February. With your family, look up information about both presidents. Then make a mini-booklet about each president. For each booklet, fold a sheet of paper into fourths. Write an interesting fact on every page.

Tell about the activity you chose. What did you like about it?

_____

_____

_____

Parent's Signature _____

Choose one activity. When it is completed, help your child dictate responses as you write them down at the bottom of the page. Return this page on the last school day of March.

1. Spiral Wind Catcher

Draw a spiral on a 9" paper square and cut it out. Decorate the spiral with crayons or markers.

Tape yarn to the center of the spiral. Hang the spiral in a place where it can move freely as it catches the wind.

2. Lucky Pot of Gold

The Irish believed that if you caught a leprechaun, you were lucky because he would lead you to his pot of gold. Talk with your family about what it means to be lucky. Then make your own "pot of gold." Cut out a large pot out of black paper. Glue the pot onto a sheet of paper. Then cut out yellow paper circles for "coins." On each coin, write one reason why you think you are lucky. Glue the coins on the paper.

I'm lucky because I have a great family.

I'm lucky because our family does fun things.

I'm lucky because I have a sister to play with.

Tell about the activity. What did you like about it?

_____

_____

_____

Parent's Signature _____

Choose one activity. When it is completed, help your child dictate responses as you write them down at the bottom of the page. Return this page on the last school day of April.

1. Celebrate Earth Day

With your family, talk about some of the problems that are affecting the environment, such as garbage disposal and pollution. Brainstorm ways that your family can help the earth. Discuss how recycling can help reduce the amount of garbage. Then plan a school lunch that uses containers and utensils that can be reused or recycled.

2. Let It Rain

Can you make rain? Try this activity and find out!

Get two clear plastic cups. Fill one cup half full of damp soil. Plant two or three bean seeds and add a little water. Place the second cup upside down on top of the first cup. Tape the cups together and place them in a sunny location. Watch what happens over the next two weeks. See if you can find "rain" anywhere!

Tell about the activity you chose. What did you like about it?

_____

_____

_____

Parent's Signature _____

39   Creative Teaching Press, Inc.

Choose one activity. When it is completed, help your child dictate responses as you write them down at the bottom of the page. Return this page on the last school day of May.

1. Mother's Day Poster

Make a poster about your mom or another special woman in your life. Draw a portrait of her in the center of a large sheet of paper. Add drawings and words around her picture to show why she is special. Present your poster on Mother's Day.

2. May Flowers

Grow some flowers from cuttings. (Cuttings of geraniums or New Guinea impatiens work well.) Experiment with the cuttings, placing some in the ground and some in containers of water. Compare the results.

Tell about the activity. What did you like about it?

_____

_____

_____

Parent's Signature _____

Choose one activity. When it is completed, help your child dictate responses as you write them down at the bottom of the page. Return this page on the last school day of June.

1. Father's Day Breakfast

With an adult's help, plan a breakfast for your dad or for another special man in your life. Find out what he likes for breakfast or give him a choice of menus. On Father's Day, deliver the breakfast with a smile. Don't forget to tell him why he is so special!

2. School Scrapbook

Gather papers, pictures, awards, and other items from the past school year. Arrange them in a scrapbook and label the various items. Include pages that tell about your favorite school memories.

Tell about the activity you chose. What did you like about it?

_____

_____

_____

Parent's Signature _____

Choose one activity. When it is completed, help your child dictate responses as you write them down at the bottom of the page. Return this page on the last school day of July.

1. Celebrate America's Birthday

Get a library book and read why America's birthday is celebrated on July the Fourth. Then celebrate this special day by making a patriotic dessert!

Ingredients:

    one box of red gelatin

    one box of blue gelatin

    one container of whipped topping

Prepare the gelatin according to directions.

Set the two kinds of gelatin in separate containers.

Later, scoop the gelatin and whipped topping into cups or glasses, alternating layers of blue gelatin, white topping, and red gelatin. Enjoy!

2. Lunar Landing

Astronauts first landed on the moon on July 20, 1969. Since then, there have been several flights to the moon! Go outside tonight and look at the moon. If you can, use binoculars to get a closer look. Draw a picture of the moon. Repeat the activity for at least seven nights. Look at the pictures to see how the moon changes during the week. Bring your drawings to school and share them with the class.

Tell about the activity. What did you like about it?

_____

_____

_____

Parent's Signature _____

Choose one activity. When it is completed, help your child dictate responses as you write them down at the bottom of the page. Return this page on the last school day of August.

1. Dream Vacation

Suppose you could have the perfect summer vacation. Think about where you would go and what you would do. Then cut out a large cloud shape from white paper. On the cloud, draw a picture showing your ideas.

2. Get Ready for School

Make a list of items you will need for school. Check store ads for specials on school supplies. Compare the prices. With a felt marker or a highlighter, mark at least five items you think are good buys.

Tell about the activity you chose. What did you like about it?

_____

_____

_____

Parent's Signature _____

Choose one activity. When it is completed, help your child dictate responses as you write them down at the bottom of the page. Return this page on the last school day of the month.

1. A Family Event

Choose a special family event, such as a birthday, graduation, or wedding. Keep a record of that special time and create a page of memories. Have each family member write a sentence telling his or her thoughts and feelings about the event. Draw a colorful border around the page, showing symbols and objects that remind you of the event.

2. Celebration Potpourri

Have each family member tell which holiday or special event is his or her favorite and why. Then plan a "potpourri party" for which people make contributions that represent their choices. For example, family members can contribute construction paper placemats decorated with holiday pictures, paper plates that come in holiday colors, birthday balloons, or napkin rings cut from toilet paper tubes and decorated with holiday stickers. Include party games with themes that reflect the different holidays or special events: Have an Easter egg hunt with real or plastic eggs. Play volleyball with birthday balloons. Put together a heart-shaped puzzle. Make words out of the letters in *Halloween*.

Tell about the activity. What did you like about it?

_____

_____

_____

Parent's Signature _____

Fun With Short Vowels

Fun With Short Vowels homework is designed with a variety of interesting activities that reinforce children's ability to discriminate short vowel sounds. Each vowel is presented on two pages. The first page provides oral exercises that develop children's ability to hear the vowel sound. The second page gives children practice in reading and writing words containing a particular vowel.

As you teach short vowels in the classroom, choose the appropriate Fun With Short Vowels homework page for students. Simply fill in the number of activities that must be completed and the due date for turning in the paper before reproducing the page for your class. Of course, many eager learners may want to do all the activities!

45

Listening Fun With Short a

Have your child complete at least _____ of the following activities. Check the appropriate box each time an activity is completed. Return this paper to school by

_____.

☐ Walk around your home. Explore inside and outside. Look for things that have a short *a* sound (such as plants, glasses, lamps, apples, and vans). How many items did you find? _____

☐ Name five words that rhyme with *cat*.

☐ Cut out magazine pictures of at least three things that have a short *a* sound. Glue the pictures onto a sheet of paper.

☐ Say five people's names that have a short *a* sound.

☐ Sit and listen while an adult calls out the words below. Stand up whenever you hear a word with short *a*.

    ham   hit   stand   name   back   top   rag   last   pan

☐ Think of a rhyming word for each of these words: *bag, pack, dad, hand*.

☐ Sing "Mary Had a Little Lamb." Then sing it again, but replace the word *lamb* with another word that has a short *a* sound. Change the last line in the song to describe your new choice.

☐ Play this game with a partner. Think of an object that has short *a* in its name. Draw a picture of it and have your partner guess what it is. Then switch roles.

Parent's Signature _____

Name _____

Writing Fun With Short a

Have your child complete at least _____ of the following activities. Check the appropriate box each time an activity is completed. Return this paper to school by _____.

☐ Use magnetic letters to build short *a* words on your refrigerator. First make the word *man*. Then change the first letter to make these words: *can, fan, ran, van*.

☐ Write a beginning letter on each line to make short *a* words:

___ag   ___ad   ___ap   ___am

☐ Cut out five apples from colored paper. On each one, write a word that has short *a*. Make a mobile by connecting the apples with yarn and tape. Make a loop at the top for hanging.

☐ Listen to an adult say the following short *a* words: *pan, bat, sad, ham, tap*. Then listen again. This time, write each word as it is called.

☐ Write the answers to these riddles. Each answer has a short *a* sound.

This animal looks like a big mouse. _____

This means the opposite of happy. _____

This is used for hitting a baseball. _____

☐ Copy the sentence below. Then circle all the rhyming words.

A fat cat sat on a mat.

_____

☐ Make a picture chart of short *a* words. First, fold a sheet of paper into four sections. Then in each section, draw a picture of something that has short *a* in its name. Label each picture.

Parent's Signature _____

Listening Fun With Short i

Have your child complete at least _____ of the following activities. Check the appropriate box each time an activity is completed. Return this paper to school by _____.

☐ Walk around your home. Explore inside and outside. Look for things that have a short *i* sound (such as pins, kittens, dishes, windows, sticks, kids). How many items did you find? _____

☐ Name five words that rhyme with *lick*.

☐ Draw pictures of at least three things that have a short *i* sound.

☐ Sit and listen while an adult calls out the words below. Stand up whenever you hear a word with short *i*.

fix   him   sat   lift   dog   hill   limp   jug   six

☐ Think of a rhyming word for each of these words: *sit, big, hip, pin*.

☐ These action words have short *i*: *kick, limp, mix, lift*. Say each word and act out its meaning.

☐ Play this game with a partner. Think of an object that has short *i* in its name. Have your partner ask yes-and-no questions to guess what it is. Then switch roles.

☐ Listen while someone says the sentence below three times. Each time, complete the sentence by saying a different word that has a short *i* sound:

Jack and Jill went up the hill to fetch a pail of _____.

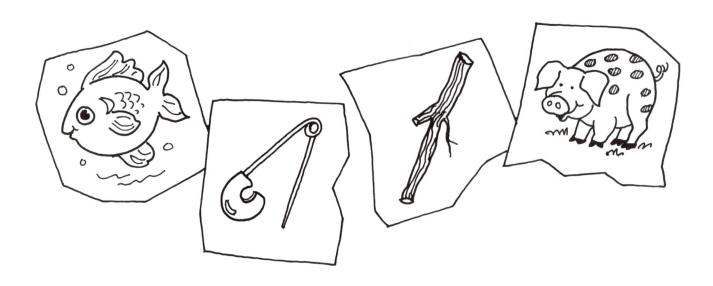

Parent's Signature _____

Name _____

Writing Fun With Short i

Have your child complete at least _____ of the following activities. Check the appropriate box each time an activity is completed. Return this paper to school by

_____.

☐ Use magnetic letters to build short *i* words on your refrigerator. First make the word *sit*. Then change the first letter to make these words: *bit, fit, hit, kit, pit.*

☐ Write a beginning letter on each line to make short *i* words:

  ___ill   ___in   ___ig   ___ip

☐ Cut out five fish from colored paper. On each one, write a word that has short *i*. Glue your fish onto paper that has been cut in the shape of a fishbowl.

☐ Listen to an adult say the following short *i* words: *him, lid, fix, did, win.* Then listen again. This time, write each word as it is called.

☐ Write the answers to these riddles. Each answer has a short *i* sound.

  This number comes after five. _____

  This animal is pink and has a curly tail. _____

  This is what you do in a chair. _____

☐ Write a sentence using all these words: *big, pig, jig.*

  _____

☐ Make a booklet of short *i* words. Fold a sheet of paper in half twice. On each page, draw a picture of something that has short *i* in its name. Label each picture.

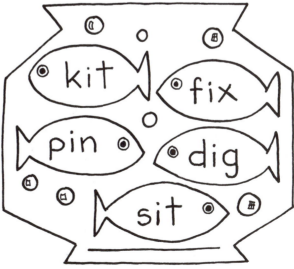

Parent's Signature _____

Listening Fun With Short o

Have your child complete at least _____of the following activities. Check the appropriate box each time an activity is completed. Return this paper to school by _____.

☐ Walk around your home. Explore inside and outside. Look for things that have a short o sound (such as dolls, boxes, dogs, socks, mops). How many items did you find? _____

☐ Cut out magazine pictures of at least three things that have a short o sound. Glue the pictures onto a sheet of paper that has been cut into the shape of an o.

☐ Sit and listen while an adult calls out the words below. Clap whenever you hear a word with short o.

     cap   hot   kick   sock   dog   mat   jog   pin   doll

☐ Think of a rhyming word for each of these words: *pot, hop, log, rock.*

☐ These animal words have short o: *dog, fox, frog, octopus.* Say each word and act like the animal.

☐ Play this game with a partner. Roll a pair of socks into a ball and toss the ball back and forth. Each time you catch the ball, you must say a word that has short o. Keep playing for at least two minutes.

☐ Listen while someone says the sentence below three times. Each time, complete the sentence by saying a different word that has a short o sound:

    Oscar found a box full of _____.

Parent's Signature _____

Name _____

Writing Fun With Short o

Have your child complete at least _____ of the following activities. Check the appropriate box each time an activity is completed. Return this paper to school by _____.

☐ Use magnetic letters to build short o words on your refrigerator. First make the word *dot*. Then change the first letter to make these words: *got, hot, not, pot.*

☐ Write a beginning letter on each line to make short o words:

___op   ___og   ___ock   ___ox

☐ Cut out four socks from colored paper. On each one, write a word that has short o. Glue a length of yarn around each sock for a colorful border.

☐ Listen to an adult say the following short o words: *top, box, hot, rod.*

Then listen again. This time, write each word as it is called.

☐ Write the answers to these riddles. Each answer has a short o sound.

This is the opposite of cold. _____

This is the opposite of bottom. _____

This helps you clean the floor. _____

☐ Copy the sentence below. Then circle all the rhyming words.

A frog met a dog by a log.

_____

☐ Accordion-fold a 4½" x 12" piece of construction paper so that you have four sections. In each section, draw a picture of something that has short o in its name. Label each picture.

frog   pot   dot   copy   mop

Parent's Signature _____

Listening Fun With Short u

Have your child complete at least _____ of the following activities. Check the appropriate box each time an activity is completed. Return this paper to school by _____.

☐ Walk around your home. Explore inside and outside. Look for things that have a short u sound (such as cups, mustard, rugs, buns, bugs). How many items did you find? _____

☐ Name five words that rhyme with jump.

☐ Think of at least three things that have a short u sound. Draw their pictures on a sheet of paper that has been cut into the shape of a u.

☐ Sit and listen while an adult calls out the words below. Jump up whenever you hear a word with short u.

cup   pick   luck   top   sun   gum   doll   duck   cap   bus

☐ Think of a rhyming word for each of these words: bug, nut, fun, rub.

☐ These action words have short u: jump, run, tug, rub. Say each word and act out its meaning.

☐ Play this game with a partner. Think of an object that has short u in its name. Give clues until your partner guesses what it is. Then switch roles.

☐ Listen while someone says the sentence below three times. Each time, complete the sentence by saying a different word that has a short u sound:

Uncle Russ has a duck that likes _____.

Parent's Signature _____

Writing Fun With Short u

Have your child complete at least _____ of the following activities. Check the appropriate box each time an activity is completed. Return this paper to school by _____.

☐ Use magnetic letters to build short u words on your refrigerator. First make the word *rug*. Then change the first letter to make these words: *dug, hug, jug, mug, tug.*

☐ Write a beginning letter on each line to make short u words:

    ___un   ___up   ___ump   ___uck

☐ Cut out five ovals from colored paper. On each one, write a word that has a short u sound. Glue the ovals onto a sheet of paper. Draw heads, legs, and other features to turn each oval into a bug.

☐ Listen to an adult say the following short u words: *bus, sun, nut, hum, tub.* Then listen again. This time, write each word as it is called.

☐ Write the answers to these riddles. Each answer has a short u sound.

This shines in the sky. _____

This animal says "quack." _____

This is something you can ride to school. _____

☐ Copy the sentence below. Then circle all the rhyming words.

It is fun to run in the sun.

_____

☐ Make a collage of short u words. Cut out the words from newspapers and magazines, and glue them onto a sheet of paper. Also cut out separate letters and glue them onto the paper to form your own short u words.

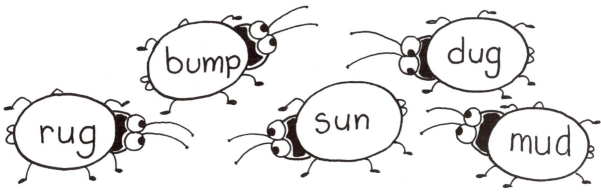

Parent's Signature _____

Listening Fun With Short e

Have your child complete at least _____ of the following activities. Check the appropriate box each time an activity is completed. Return this paper to school by _____ .

☐ Walk around your home. Explore inside and outside. Look for things that have a short e sound (such as eggs, beds, envelopes, pennies, and webs). How many items did you find? _____

☐ Name five words that rhyme with *pet*.

☐ Use a red crayon or marker to draw at least three things that have a short e sound.

☐ Listen while an adult calls out the words below. Put your hands on your head whenever you hear a word with short *e*.

     pen   red   van   net   lost   men   fun   tent   jump

☐ Think of a rhyming word for each of these words: *hen, fed, went, vest*.

☐ Say five people's names that have a short e sound.

☐ Play this game with a partner. Think of an object that has short e in its name. Draw a picture of it and have your partner guess what it is. Then switch roles.

☐ Listen while someone says the sentence below three times. Each time, complete the sentence by saying a different word that has a short e sound:

    Jenny sent Peggy ten red _____ .

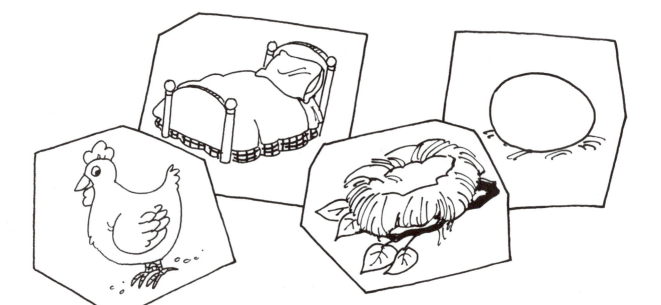

Parent's Signature _____

Writing Fun With Short e

Have your child complete at least _____ of the following activities. Check the appropriate box each time an activity is completed. Return this paper to school by _____.

☐ Use magnetic letters to build short e words on your refrigerator. First make the word *hen*. Then change the first letter to make these words: *men, pen, ten*.

☐ Write a beginning letter on each line to make short e words:

___et   ___ed   ___ell   ___est

☐ Cut out five eggs from white paper. On each one, write a word that has short e. Draw a large nest on a sheet of paper. Color the nest. Then glue the eggs onto the nest.

☐ Listen to an adult say the following short e words: *wet, web, hem, leg, bed*. Then listen again. This time, write each word as it is called.

☐ Write the answers to these riddles. Each answer has a short e sound.

This number comes after nine. _____

This is what people sleep on. _____

This is what a spider spins. _____

☐ Write a sentence using all these words: *Ted, red, bed*.

_____

☐ Make a picture chart of short e words. First, fold a sheet of paper into four sections. Then in each section, draw a picture of something that has short e in its name. Label each picture.

Parent's Signature _____

55

Review Short Vowels

Have your child complete and check off at least _____ of the following activities. Return this paper to school by _____.

☐ Listen to someone say these words: *bag, cup, pin, bed, rock*. Then listen again. This time, say the vowel you hear in each word.

☐ Make a Short Vowels booklet. Staple five sheets of paper together. Label the first page **Short a**, the second page **Short i**, the third page **Short o**, the fourth page **Short u**, and the fifth page **Short e**. Glue on magazine pictures or make drawings for each page.

☐ Copy this sentence and underline all the short vowels:

Tom will get a puppy.

_____

☐ Write a different vowel on each line. Then read the words.

b __ g   b __ g   b __ g

☐ Write a sentence. Try to use as many words as you can that have short vowels. Then circle those words.

_____

_____

☐ Make a Short Vowels caterpillar. Cut out paper ovals. On each oval, write a word that has a short vowel. Glue the ovals together. Add one oval for the face.

Parent's Signature _____

Across the Curriculum

Real-life learning by its very nature crosses the curriculum. Across the Curriculum homework pages are designed to reinforce classroom learning in language arts, math, science, social studies, art, music, drama, and physical education. These activities offer children the opportunity to successfully follow each task through to completion and to develop the problem-solving skills so important in everyday life.

Each Across the Curriculum page begins with a section informing parents of the purpose of the homework. Easy-to-implement activity directions follow. The activities utilize simple items found in most households.

Before duplicating the homework page, simply fill in the due date. Ask children to bring back each of the completed projects or homework pages by the date you have filled in.

Alphabet Scavenger Hunt

Help your child complete this assignment. Turn it in by _____.

When a child finds and names letters of the alphabet, he or she is learning

- to become aware of print in the world around him or her.
- to recognize and name letters.
- to sequence letters.

Activity

1. Review the alphabet by singing the "Alphabet Song" with a family member.

2. Go on a scavenger hunt around your home. Look for letters of the alphabet on food labels, books, and household items. Try to find as many letters of the alphabet, from *a* to *z*, as you can.

3. Keep track of the letters found by listing them on the lines below.

_____

_____

_____

_____

_____

Variation: Play Alphabet Scavenger Hunt during a car trip. Look for letters on license plates, signs, and billboards.

Parent's Signature _____

Grocery Store Game

Help your child complete this assignment. Turn it in by _____.

When a child thinks of words and beginning sounds, he or she is learning

- that letters are associated with sounds.
- that words are made up of letters and sounds.
- that many words begin with the same sound.

Activity

1. Play this game with your family. The first player thinks of an item that is sold at a grocery store. That person says, *I went to the grocery store and bought something that begins with the letter _____*.

2. The other players take turns naming grocery items that begin with that letter. The player who correctly guesses the item gets to select the next item.

3. Keep playing until everyone has had a chance to select an item.

   Tell about the activity. What did you like about the game?

   _____

   _____

   _____

Parent's Signature _____

     59

A Tasty Sandwich

Help your child complete this assignment. Turn it in by _____.

When a child practices giving directions, he or she is learning

- to sequence tasks.
- to think logically.
- to be clear and specific with language.

Activity

How good are you at giving directions? Try this activity and find out!

1. Ask an adult to help you get out the ingredients and utensils you will need to make a peanut butter and jelly sandwich.

2. Step by step, give directions for making the sandwich. See that the person listening to you follows your directions exactly.

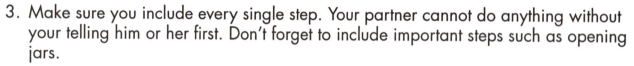

3. Make sure you include every single step. Your partner cannot do anything without your telling him or her first. Don't forget to include important steps such as opening jars.

4. Once the sandwich is finished, congratulate each other. Then enjoy the sandwich together!

Tell about the activity. What did you like about it?

_____

_____

_____

Parent's Signature _____

Storybook Diorama

Help your child complete this assignment. Turn it in by _____.

When a child presents a story through a diorama, he or she is learning

- to interpret the setting of a story.
- to identify main characters.
- to select a favorite event.

Activity

1. Read a story with a family member.
2. Talk about the setting (when and where the story takes place). Name the main characters and tell what they did in the story. Tell about your favorite part of the story.
3. Make a shoebox diorama showing the part of the story you liked best. First, paint a scene showing where the story takes place. Then add small objects such as rocks, twigs, and toy figures to the scene. Make drawings of characters or objects and tape them to the scene, too.
4. Bring the diorama to school and share it with the class.

Parent's Signature _____

Secret Writing Pals

Help your child complete this assignment. Turn it in by _____.

When a child writes a note complimenting a secret pal, he or she is learning

- to write sentences.
- to express feelings on paper.
- to develop handwriting skills.

Activity

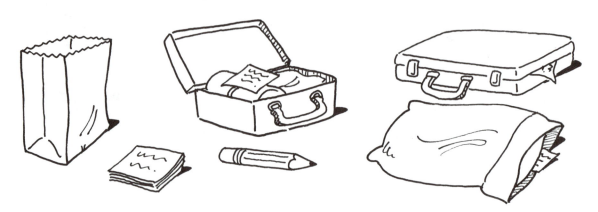

1. Write the name of each family member on a separate piece of paper.
2. Fold the papers and put them in a brown paper bag.
3. Each family member draws a name from the bag. The name drawn becomes that person's secret writing pal.
4. Each person writes a note to his or her secret writing pal. The note should tell why that secret pal is special. Leave the note unsigned.
5. Each writer secretly places the note in a place where his or her secret writing pal can find it, such as on a pillow, in a briefcase, or in a lunch box.

Tell about the activity. What did you like about it?

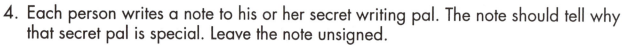

_____

Parent's Signature _____

Some Up, Some Down

Help your child complete this assignment. Turn it in by _____.

When a child forms number sentences involving addition, he or she is learning

- to understand that addition results from combining groups.
- to see that sums can be made up of different combinations of groups.
- to develop computation skills.

Activity

Play this game with a family member or friend.

1. Get five pennies. Toss them onto a table.

2. Check to see how many coins come up heads and how many come up tails. On the back of this paper, write a number sentence to show the results. (Example: 2 + 3 = 5)

3. Let your partner have the next throw. Write the matching number sentence below the first one.

4. Continue the activity until you have at least six number sentences.

5. Look at the number sentences you wrote. Which one occurred more times than the others? _____

Variations:

- Use more than five coins.

- Make subtraction sentences. (Example: If you toss five coins and three of them land heads-up, you could write 5 – 3 = 2.)

Parent's Signature _____

Card Sharks

Help your child complete this assignment. Turn it in by _____.

When a child adds the numbers on playing cards, he or she is learning

- to see addition as a form of combining groups.
- to see sums as different combinations of groups.
- to compare sums.

Activity

Play this addition game with a family member or friend.

1. Remove the face cards from a deck of cards.

2. Shuffle the remaining cards and place them in a pile facedown.

3. The first player picks up two cards, looks at the numbers, and says a number sentence stating the sum. For example, if the cards are 3 and 4, the player says *3 plus 4 equals 7.*

4. The second player picks up two cards and repeats the procedure.

5. The player who has the greater sum keeps all four cards. The next round continues with the players repeating steps 3 and 4.

6. If both players have the same sum, the players each pick up another card and add it to their pile. The player who has the greater sum wins the round.

7. Keep playing until all the cards have been played. The player who wins the most rounds wins the game.

Tell about the activity. What did you like about it?

_____

_____

_____

Parent's Signature _____

Share a Sandwich

Help your child complete this assignment. Turn it in by _____.

When a child cuts sandwiches into fractional parts, he or she is learning

- to divide a whole into parts.
- to make parts equal in size.
- the names of fractional parts.

Activity

1. Make two sandwiches with an adult. (Cheese or peanut butter works best.)

2. With a butter knife, cut one sandwich into two equal parts.

3. Look at the sandwich. Are the parts the same or different in size? _____

   When one thing is divided into two equal parts, each part is called *one-half*.

4. Cut the other sandwich into four equal parts.

5. Look at the sandwich. Are the parts the same or different in size? _____

   When one thing is divided into four equal parts, each part is called *one-fourth*.

6. Place two-fourths of a sandwich on top of one-half of a sandwich. What do you

   notice? _____

   _____

Parent's Signature _____

A One-Handed Clock

Help your child complete this assignment. Turn it in by _____.

When a child practices telling time by the hour, he or she is learning

- that a clock is a way of measuring time.
- that time can by measured in hours.
- that the shorter hand on a clock identifies the hour.

Activity

Did you know that you can figure out the time even if your clock only has an hour hand? This activity shows you how!

1. Ask an adult to help you make a paper clock. Get a large paper plate and write the numbers *1* to *12* around it. Make a short hour hand by cutting an arrow from paper.

2. Point the hand exactly at the *4*. The clock shows 4 o'clock. Then point the clock exactly at the *5*. What time do you think the clock shows? ____ o'clock

3. Move the hour hand to different numbers and tell what time it is.

4. Point the hand exactly at the *4* again. Then move it slightly past the *4*. The clock shows that it is a little after 4 o'clock. Move the hand halfway between the *4* and *5*. The clock shows that it is after 4 o'clock but before ___ o'clock.

5. Point the hand just before the *5*. The clock shows that it is almost ___ o'clock.

6. Keep working with your partner. Move the hour hand slightly past or slightly before different numbers and tell what time it is. (*It's a little after ____. It's almost ___ o'clock.*)

7. Look at a real clock every so often during the day. Focus on the hour hand. Say what time it is. (*It's ___ o'clock. It's a little after ___.*

   It's almost ___ o'clock.)

Parent's Signature _____

What Will You Wear?

Help your child complete this assignment. Turn it in by _____.

When a child combines clothes to make different outfits, he or she is learning
- to see a variety of possible combinations.
- to keep a record of the combinations made.
- to develop problem-solving skills.

Activity

1. Choose two tops (shirts or blouses) and two bottoms (pants, shorts, or skirts).

2. Think of as many ways as you can to combine the tops and bottoms. Move the clothes around to make the combinations.

3. Draw the different combinations in the box below. Color the clothes so that they match your clothing.

How many different outfits did you make? _____

Extension: Repeat the activity with three tops and three bottoms. Draw your outfits on the back of this paper.

Parent's Signature _____

Measure and Play

Help your child complete this assignment. Turn it in by _____.

When a child measures rice or pasta, he or she is learning

- to measure.
- to understand the concept of fractions.
- to see the relationship between a whole and its fractional parts.

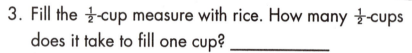

Activity

1. Get four measuring cups:
   1-cup, $\frac{1}{2}$-cup, $\frac{1}{3}$-cup, and $\frac{1}{4}$-cup.

2. Pour some uncooked rice (or pasta) in a tub or large bowl.

3. Fill the $\frac{1}{2}$-cup measure with rice. How many $\frac{1}{2}$-cups does it take to fill one cup? _____

4. Repeat step 3, using the $\frac{1}{3}$-cup measure. How many $\frac{1}{3}$-cups does it take to fill one cup? _____

5. Repeat step 3, using the $\frac{1}{4}$-cup measure. How many $\frac{1}{4}$-cups does it take to fill one cup? _____

6. Fill the 1-cup measure with rice. Pour the rice into the $\frac{1}{2}$-cup measure. If the cup gets full, empty it out. How many times can you fill the $\frac{1}{2}$-cup measure until the 1-cup measure has no rice left? _____

7. Repeat step 6, using the 1-cup measure and the $\frac{1}{3}$-cup measure. How many times can you fill the $\frac{1}{3}$-cup measure? _____

8. Repeat step 6, using the 1-cup measure and the $\frac{1}{4}$-cup measure. How many times can you fill the $\frac{1}{4}$-cup measure? _____

Parent's Signature _____

How Much Money?

Help your child complete this assignment. Turn it in by _____.

When a child counts coins, he or she is learning

- to name coins.
- to associate value with coins.
- to count by ones, fives, and tens.

(Note to Parents: For this activity, it is especially important that you work with your child at his or her level. Understanding comes with lots of practice. Increase the difficulty of the activity only when your child shows that he or she is ready.)

Activity

Do you know the value of different combinations of coins? Find out with this activity.

You will need ten pennies, ten nickels, and ten dimes.

- **Count Pennies**
  Lay out ten pennies on a table. Count them by ones.
  How many cents do you have? _____ cents

- **Count Nickels**
  Lay out ten nickels on a table. Count them by fives.
  How many cents do you have? _____ cents

- **Count Dimes**
  Lay out ten dimes on a table. Count them by tens.
  How many cents do you have? _____ cents

- **Count Pennies, Nickels, and Dimes**
  Lay out a penny, a nickel, and a dime.
  How many cents do you have? _____ cents

Ask an adult to lay out different groups of pennies, nickels, and dimes. Each time, tell how many cents you have.

Parent's Signature _____

My Shadow

Help your child complete this assignment. Turn it in by _____.

When a child measures a shadow, he or she is learning

- that a shadow is caused by the blocking of sunlight.
- that the size of a shadow varies with the time of day.
- that the position of the sun determines the length of the shadow.

Activity

1. Go outside in the morning on a sunny day. Stand on a paved area with your back to the sun. Your shadow will fall in front of you.

2. Have an adult trace your shadow with chalk. Also have your feet traced so that you can tell where you were standing.

3. Repeat the activity at noon and in the afternoon. Each time, position your feet in the same place. Each shadow should be traced with a different color of chalk.

4. How did the shadows change? What do you think caused the changes?

_____

_____

_____

_____

_____

Parent's Signature _____

Sail Away!

Help your child complete this assignment. Turn it in by _____.

When a child makes a cardboard sailboat, he or she is learning
- that some objects float.
- that some materials resist water better than others.
- that moving air moves objects.

Activity

Make a boat that really floats!

1. Cut a 3" x 4" piece of cardboard for the bottom of the boat.

2. Color one side of the cardboard with crayon. Press heavily.

3. Cut out a sail from drawing paper and poke a toothpick through it.

4. Tape the toothpick to the uncolored side of the cardboard.

5. Place the boat in a sink or tub full of water. Blow on the sail and watch what happens!

6. Think about how you made your boat. Why do you think the side of the cardboard that is covered with crayon is placed in the water?

_____

_____

7. What happened to the boat when you blew on the sail? Why did this happen?

_____

_____

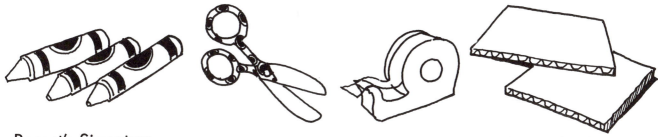

Parent's Signature _____

Seed Hunt

Help your child complete this assignment. Turn it in by _____.

When a child examines seeds, he or she is learning

- that many plants have seeds.
- that seeds vary in size, shape, and color.
- that seeds grow into plants.

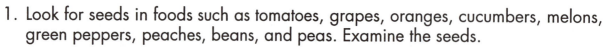

Activity

1. Look for seeds in foods such as tomatoes, grapes, oranges, cucumbers, melons, green peppers, peaches, beans, and peas. Examine the seeds.

2. Talk with your family about the seeds. Tell how the seeds are similar and how they are different.

3. Draw four kinds of seeds in the boxes below. Label each seed.

Extension: Plant some of the seeds in a pot or in the ground. Watch what happens for one or two weeks.

Parent's Signature _____

Name _____

Mixing Colors

Help your child complete this assignment. Turn it in by _____.

When a child mixes colors, he or she is learning

- that colors can change.
- that two colors combine to form a new color.
- that colors can change in intensity.

Activity

1. Cover a table with newspaper. Set out six small jars.
   Fill three of the jars half full of water.

2. Add two drops of red food coloring to the first jar. Add yellow food coloring to the second jar and blue food coloring to the third jar.

3. Stir the water in each jar to mix in the color completely.

4. Pour some red water and some yellow water into an empty jar. Stir to mix. What happens? _____

5. Mix some yellow water and blue water in an empty jar. What happens?

   _____

6. Mix some red water and blue water in an empty jar. What happens?

   _____

7. What happens when you add more red water to the mixture of red and yellow water?

   _____

8. What happens when you add more yellow water to the mixture of yellow and blue water?

   _____

9. What happens when you add more blue water to the mixture of red and blue water?

   _____

Parent's Signature _____

Personal Quilt

Help your child complete this assignment. Turn it in by _____.

When a child designs a personal quilt, he or she is learning
- to think about important events in his or her life.
- to communicate events through pictures.
- to develop self-worth.

Activity

1. Choose six important events in your life. (Examples: birth, learning to walk, losing your first baby tooth, first day of school)

2. Get a 12" x 18" sheet of paper. Divide it into six sections.

3. Draw an important event in each section. Label each picture.

4. Bring your quilt to school and share it with the class.

   Variation: Draw your pictures with markers on felt squares and sew them together.

born | learned to walk | lost first tooth
riding a bike | learned to read | went to Hawaii

Parent's Signature _____

Family Chores

Help your child complete this assignment. Turn it in by _____.

When a child lists household chores, he or she is learning
- to identify responsibilities in the home.
- to think of ways family members work together.
- to appreciate the importance of each family member.

Activity

1. With your family, list the chores that have to get done to keep the home running smoothly.
2. Beside each chore, write the name(s) of the people who help get that chore done.
3. Draw one star beside the chores that you do.
4. Draw two stars beside the chores that you have never done but that you think you can learn to do.
5. Make a thank-you note to your parents and other members of the family for all the work they do.

Parent's Signature _____

Having Fun Then and Now

Help your child complete this assignment. Turn it in by _____.

When a child finds out how different generations lived, he or she is learning

- to compare how lifestyles change over the years.
- to conduct interviews.
- to record information.

Activity

1. Write your name at the top of a sheet of paper. Then list the fun things you like to do either alone or with friends. Add pictures if you like. At the bottom of the paper, write *Having Fun in ____,* and complete the title with the year.

2. Interview your mom or dad. Ask your parent to name the fun things he or she did at your age. Write those things on a sheet of paper that has been labeled with your mom or dad's name at the top. At the bottom, write *Having Fun in _____,* and complete the title with the year your parent was your age.

3. If you can, interview a grandparent or another older person. Repeat the activity described in step 2.

4. Tape the papers together so that you can look at them all at once.

5. Share your work with your class.

Parent's Signature _____

Family Sing-along

Help your child complete this assignment. Turn it in by_____.

When a child experiments with a song, he or she is learning

- to carry a tune.
- to keep time to music.
- to be creative in musical expression.

Activity

1. As a family, sing "Row, Row, Row Your Boat."
2. Hum the tune together.
3. Sing the song again, but this time clap out the rhythm of the song.
4. Clap out the rhythm without singing aloud. Instead, everyone should "sing" silently in their heads as they clap along.
5. Break up into two or three groups. Sing the song in rounds.
6. Choose other songs to sing, hum, and clap.

   Tell about the activity. What did you like about it?

_____

_____

_____

Parent's Signature _____

Here Comes the Rhythm Band!

Help your child complete this assignment. Turn it in by _____.

When a child uses rhythm instruments, he or she is learning

- to keep time to music.
- to experiment with sound.
- to be creative in musical expression.

Activity

1. Have each family member select one or more household objects to use as rhythm instruments. For example, two wooden spoons could be used for rhythm sticks, two pot lids for cymbals, a pot and a wooden spoon for a drum and drumstick, and a plastic container of seeds or beans for a shaker.

2. Experiment with the instruments to find ways to make different sounds.

3. Take turns playing different instruments while the others listen.

4. Put on some lively music. Then have the whole family accent the rhythm with the instruments.

Tell about the activity. What did you like about it?

_____

_____

_____

Parent's Signature _____

Look and Sketch

Help your child complete this assignment. Turn it in by _____.

When a child practices sketching, he or she is learning
- to observe carefully and notice details.
- to develop hand-eye coordination.
- to appreciate beauty in the environment.

Activity

1. Ask a family member or friend to join you outside with a pencil and a sketch pad. If you do not have a sketch pad, use a sheet of drawing paper and a hard-covered book for support.

2. Find an interesting subject, sit down in a comfortable position, and begin drawing. Don't worry about making the lines perfect.

3. As you study your subject, think about these questions:
   - Do I see any straight lines or curved lines?
   - Does the subject look long, thin, wide, or short?
   - Do I see anything that looks like a circle, rectangle, square, or triangle?

4. Bring your sketch to school and share it with the class.

Parent's Signature _____

79

Creative Teaching Press, Inc.

Kitchen Mosaic

Help your child complete this assignment. Turn it in by _____.

When a child makes a mosaic, he or she is learning

- to work with three-dimensional objects.
- to select materials that express his or her ideas.
- to appreciate color, shape, and texture.

Activity

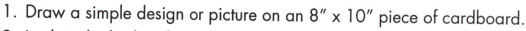

A mosaic is a picture or design made by fitting small pieces of materials together. You can make an interesting mosaic using things from your kitchen!

1. Draw a simple design or picture on an 8" x 10" piece of cardboard.
2. Look in the kitchen for some materials that can be used to fill in your design or picture. Some ideas include: pasta, beans, popcorn, cereal, rice, and dried split peas.
3. Glue the materials to the cardboard. Cover as much of the cardboard as you can. You may need several days to complete your mosaic.
4. When the glue is dry, tape a loop of yarn to the back for hanging.

Parent's Signature _____

Family Theater

Help your child complete this assignment. Turn it in by _____.

When a child acts out a story, he or she is learning

- to sequence story events.
- to think creatively.
- to perform in front of others.

Activity

1. Read a story with your family. Choose a fairy tale or another story that has several characters and interesting dialogue.

2. Make a plan for acting out the story. Work together to write the script, choose the players for the different characters, and make the props or costumes. Plan your performance below.

_____

_____

_____

_____

_____

_____

_____

_____

_____

_____

_____

_____

3. When everything is ready, perform the play! Lights! Camera! Action!

Parent's Signature _____

81

Fun With Puppets

Help your child complete this assignment. Turn it in by _____.

When a child puts on a puppet show, he or she is learning

- to sequence events.
- to remember story dialogue.
- to perform in front of others.

Activity

Put on a puppet play with your family.

1. Read a fairy tale or another story with your family.
2. Make stick puppets of the different characters by drawing the characters on paper and taping a craft stick to each one.
3. Write a script for the puppet play. Practice moving the puppets and saying your lines.
4. Use a large box, a sofa, or a table turned on its side for the puppet theater.
5. Present the play to your family.

   Tell about the activity. What did you like about it?

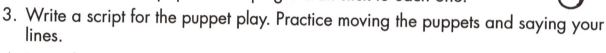

_____

_____

Parent's Signature _____

Name

Keep to the Beat!

Help your child complete this assignment. Turn it in by _____.

When a child exercises to music, he or she is learning

- to move to music.
- to keep a steady beat.
- to use a variety of body movements.

Activity

1. Wear comfortable clothes and play some lively music. Then exercise to the beat. Move freely to the music. Here are some ideas:

   - Move your arms up, down, and to the side.

   - Twist your body from side to side.

   - Walk in place.

   - Take two or three steps to the left and then to the right.

2. After everyone has had a chance to warm up for five or ten minutes, have each person take a turn leading the others. The leader can try such exercises as jumping jacks, marching, running in place, or kicking.

3. After everyone has been a leader, start warming down. Walk around the room at a medium pace for a few minutes. If you like, play some slow music and move your body gently to the rhythm. Hold your hands over your head and stretch your body, rotating slowly from your left side to your back, from your back to your right side, and from your right side towards your front. Then stretch around the other way.

Parent's Signature _____

Jumping Fun

Help your child complete this assignment. Turn it in by _____.

When a child jumps rope, he or she is learning

- to jump with a steady rhythm.
- to develop coordination.
- to take pleasure from physical exercise.

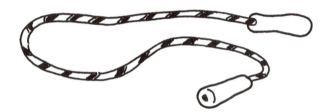

Activity

1. Lay a long jump rope across the floor. Jump back and forth over the still rope.

2. Tie a long rope to a doorknob. Ask a parent or an older sibling to turn the rope for you as you jump. Have a partner hold your hands and jump with you.

3. Try jumping alone while someone turns the rope for you. Count how many times you can jump without stepping on the rope.

Variations:

- Have two people stand and hold the ends of the jump rope. Have them gently swing the rope back and forth close to the ground. Jump back and forth over the rope.

- Lay the rope on the ground. Have two people squat and hold the ends of the jump rope. Have the people wiggle the rope back and forth to form waves. Then jump back and forth over the waves.

Which jumping method did you like the best? Why? _____

Tell about the activity. What did you like about the game?

_____

_____

_____

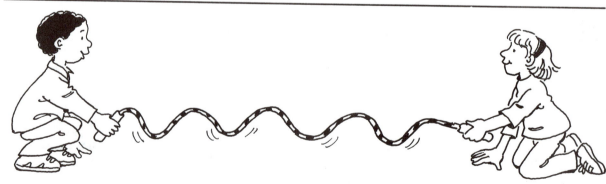

Parent's Signature _____

Family Adventures

A trip to an airport . . . or a trip to a parent's workplace? Family Adventure homework pages invite students and their families to go on real-life or make-believe adventures together. And naturally, families learn as they go! These real-life experiences will develop creative and critical thinking skills as well as enhance learning in reading, writing, social studies, and science.

Each homework page begins with an idea for an adventure. There is always the possibility of turning a real-life adventure into a make-believe one if the family is unable to go by saying "Let's pretend we went to . . ."

When assigning a Family Adventure, fill in the due date at the top of the page and write the number of activities to be completed before duplicating the page for each child. Discuss the page with the class and then send it home. Families discuss the activities and choose the ones they want to do. As each activity is completed, the corresponding box is checked off. Children return the page to school by the due date.

Transportation Adventure

Help your child complete this assignment. Turn it in by _____.

As a family, visit a transportation center such as an airport, a train depot, a bus station, or a harbor. Complete and check off at least _____ of the following activities.

☐ Observe the different kinds of workers. List who they are and what you think they do.

☐ Find a schedule that lists arrivals and departures. Write the names of three places people are traveling to and the names of three places they are traveling from.

☐ Close your eyes and listen carefully. Describe four things you hear.

☐ Copy two signs you see.

☐ Look around you. Estimate how many people you see.

☐ Describe one interesting sight.

☐ Write how long it takes to get from your home to the transportation center.

☐ Look for the following places. Check each place you find:

__ a place to eat   __ a place to buy gifts   __ a place to make a phone call

☐ When you get home, draw a picture of the place you visited.

Parent's Signature _____

Name _____

Backyard Adventure

Help your child complete this assignment. Turn it in by _____.

A tour of your backyard or a nearby park can be a fun learning experience. Take spoons, trowels, strainers, magnifying glasses, pencils, and sheets of paper with you. Then complete and check off at least _____ of the following activities as a family.

☐ Make a list of the different creatures in your backyard. If you don't know the names, draw their pictures instead.

☐ Make a list of the different plants in your backyard. If you don't know the names, draw their pictures instead.

☐ Scoop up some soil and examine it with a magnifying glass. Describe what you see.

☐ Scoop up some soil and put it in your strainer. Sift out the finer materials. Place the material left in your strainer on a sheet of paper. Describe what you see.

☐ Feel the top of the soil in a garden or a flower bed. Pay attention to how warm or cool it feels. Then dig a hole about six inches deep. Place your hand in the hole. How is the temperature different?

☐ Find out how many steps it takes you to go all the way around your backyard.

☐ Count the number of homes you can see from your backyard.

☐ Describe the tallest thing in your backyard.

☐ Name the activities your family enjoys doing in the backyard.

Parent's Signature _____

Grocery Store Adventure

Help your child complete this assignment. Turn it in by _____.

Plan a day when the family can go to the grocery store together. Complete and check off at least _____ of the following activities.

- ☐ List ten different things that can be bought at the store.
- ☐ Find out the store hours.
- ☐ Find three things that your family has never bought before.
- ☐ Name five nonfood items you can buy.
- ☐ Find five items that are made in other countries.
- ☐ Estimate how many apples it will take to make one pound. Weigh the apples to check your guess.
- ☐ List four seafoods you can buy.
- ☐ Read three signs in the store.
- ☐ Look for five foods that have been precooked.
- ☐ List three things that can be bought for less than a dollar.
- ☐ When you get home, draw pictures of six things your family bought.

Parent's Signature _____

Parent's Workplace Adventure

Help your child complete this assignment. Turn it in by _____.

Visiting a parent's workplace can be a wonderful learning experience! Plan to visit at a time when the parent can show the child around and introduce him or her to co-workers. Complete and check off at least _____ of the following activities.

- ☐ Write the phone number and address of the workplace.
- ☐ List your parent's main responsibilities at work.
- ☐ Find out what kind of training your parent needed for the job.
- ☐ Find out how many years your parent has worked at his or her job.
- ☐ Look on a map to see the route your parent travels to get from home to work.
- ☐ List any special equipment your parent uses at work.
- ☐ Find out where your parent goes for lunch and for breaks.
- ☐ Write the times your parent starts work, has lunch, takes breaks, and goes home.
- ☐ Talk about a job you might one day like to do at your parent's workplace.
- ☐ Ask your parent what he or she enjoys most about work.
- ☐ Introduce yourself to at least one of your parent's co-workers.
- ☐ Write one thing you learned at your parent's place of work.

Parent's Signature _____

Indoor Camping Adventure

Help your child complete this assignment. Turn it in by _____.

Turn the inside of your home into a special campsite! Set up a "tent" by draping an old sheet or blanket over a table. Then plan some fun camping activities using the ideas below. Complete and check off at least _____ of the following activities.

☐ When it gets dark, sit under the table and have someone read to the others by flashlight.

☐ Munch on some popcorn, crackers, or other tasty treats in your tent.

☐ Play a board game or a card game in your tent.

☐ Go on a hike at night. First, turn off all the lights. Then walk through your home with flashlights. Notice how the place looks without the lights on.

☐ Turn off the lights. Aim your flashlights at the ceiling. Move the flashlights or turn them on and off to create a light show.

☐ Sit in a circle on the floor and sing songs.

☐ Sit in a circle on the floor and tell stories.

☐ Make hot chocolate together.

☐ Close your eyes and listen carefully. Let everyone take turns naming one sound they hear.

☐ Sleep in sleeping bags or on blankets overnight.

☐ Write two things you enjoyed about your indoor camping adventure.

Parent's Signature _____

Timely Tips Newsletters

Timely Tips Newsletters are perfect mediums for conveying important information to your parents on such topics as homework, reading, television, and self-confidence. Parents want to be good partners in their child's education, but often lack the knowledge or confidence to deal with these issues in an effective way.

Share and discuss these Timely Tip Newsletters with parents at Open House or send them home with students at appropriate times throughout the year. You will find that your parents will appreciate this valuable support/assistance.

Homework

Timely Tips Newsletter

Did You Know?

Homework can turn into "homeplay" when you support your child and do your best to make learning at home a fun experience. Use the following tips to help your child make the most of homework experiences.

- Set a regular time and place to do the homework. Allow your child to help make this decision so she or he is part of the decision-making process.

- Help your child find a quiet and comfortable place to work. Encourage him or her to avoid interruptions. Turn off the TV.

- Provide the necessary tools such as paper, pencils, crayons, and scissors.

- When necessary, read the directions to your child and make sure they are understood.

- If necessary, demonstrate how to complete the homework before having your child try it alone.

- Whenever appropriate, sign your child's homework paper. This sends a message to the teacher that you are involved in your child's learning.

- If you have any questions regarding assignments, ask the teacher.

- Praise your child's efforts and keep the atmosphere positive.

Reading

Timely Tips Newsletter

Did You Know?

Your child will become a better learner when you are his or her partner in education. As one of the most important people in your child's life, you have an opportunity to make a critical difference in how successful your child will be in school. Reading together is one way to become your child's partner in education. Use the following tips when reading with your child.

- Read to your child every night if you can. It is one of the most important activities the two of you can share. Use the time to cuddle up together and make the reading experience loving and enjoyable.

- Remember not to turn every reading session into a lesson. Your overall goal is to provide a pleasurable reading experience.

- Choose books that are the appropriate level for your child.

- Choose books that are of interest to your child.

- Occasionally, have your child place his or her finger under each word as the two of you read.

- Ask your child to predict what will happen next at a natural point in a story.

- Ask your child if he or she liked the way the book ended. If not, ask how he or she might change it.

- Children often choose to read or listen to the same books over and over. Go for it! This repetition helps your child with vocabulary, word recognition, and story sequence, among other important skills.

- Don't worry about having your child read to you. Your child will gain more from the experience if he or she is allowed to listen and take in the story while you read.

 # Television

Timely Tips Newsletter

Did You Know?

As every parent knows, television can interfere with and delay the completion of homework. Use the following techniques to make television-viewing a more meaningful experience for your child.

- Set limits. Establish good habits by allowing your child to view TV for only an hour (or less) a day.

- Plan. Look at your local television guide and decide together which shows to watch. Talk about which ones are appropriate and at what times they should be viewed.

- Participate. Watch together the shows you choose. Discuss parts of the show and explain things when necessary. Ask your child for ideas about ways the show could have been presented differently.

- Monitor. Encourage your child to choose programs about positive and loving situations. Discuss the characters and why they do what they do.

- Analyze commercials. Help your child analyze commercials and recognize exaggerated claims.

- Seek alternatives. Instead of watching television, have your child participate in activities such as music lessons; after-school sports, programs or clubs; or at-home arts and crafts projects.

Learning on the Go

Timely Tips Newsletter

Did You Know?

The "real world" is the most natural place for your child to learn. It abounds with new and exciting educational experiences. Invite your child to learn in the real world by participating with you in some of the following activities.

- Visit community buildings and attractions such as a farm, museum, or fire station.

- Take your child on errands to the grocery store, cleaners, post office, and hardware store. Take time to browse around and talk about the different jobs people have.

- Provide free or unstructured time for your child. Invite him or her to listen to music, daydream, or learn to entertain him or herself.

- Take a train trip or a bus ride.

- Have your child obtain a library card and visit the library regularly. Set a good example for your child by checking out books for yourself as well.

- Take walks in your neighborhood.

- Go to special events such as sporting events, concerts, or movies. Try to find events that are free and age-appropriate.

- Have your child join community organizations such as the Scouts, 4-H Club, Camp Fire, soccer, or T-ball programs.

- Play a board game or do a puzzle together.

- Read signs, license plates, bumper stickers, and billboards together.

- Talk about the environment such as the colors, smells, and noises around you.

- When in the car, talk about directions, traffic rules, and what to expect next.

Building Your Child's Self-Confidence

Timely Tips Newsletter

I went to the mountains this summer.

Did You Know?

With support and guidance, every child can learn. And you can provide that support by working to build your child's self-confidence in learning. Use the following tips to help your child develop self-esteem and self-confidence.

- Praise your child every time you see something positive. Be specific about your praise by telling him or her what you like and why.

- Set realistic goals for your child.

- Be patient with your child when he or she tries something new. Remind your child that "practice makes perfect."

- Let your child learn things on his or her own whenever possible. Children spend a lot of time trying to make sense of their world.

- Display your child's creations such as drawings, paintings, and writings.

- Photograph your child engaged in a learning task and display the photos around the house.

- Encourage your child in a positive way to try again when he or she is unsuccessful or frustrated.

- Spend time together. Work, play, talk, or just be together for a little while every day.

- Through words and hugs, let your child know that you believe in him or her.

- Remind your child that it is "okay" to make mistakes.